Shouldering The Stars

Joseph Michael Lowery

ISBN: 9781687717207

For Mom, because you got through it.

CONTENTS

Contents

Contents

Contents

Contents

Contents

Contents

A DAY'S BEAUTY

when everything
finally quiets down
and when the sun
finally dims
the beauty of routine,
this systematic approach
to daily life makes
itself clear, makes
you better, brings
about happiness, makes
you finally wish
things wouldn't change,
at least for this moment
because life maybe didn't
get it perfect, but
it did get it right

ABUNDANCE

how do you feel
when you have enough?
how do you treat others?

when there's enough time
you don't rush
when you feel secure
you don't try to make
others insecure
when you're overflowing
with happiness
you only want
to reflect that outward
and give it away

what if we took that feeling
and used it even
when feeling low?

how would that change us?
would we still pollute
each other with negative
words and actions?

would we still hate?
or would there finally
be room for understanding
and love?

AGENDA

don't be fooled
everyone's got
an agenda
but you don't
have to give up
on people
quite yet

ALREADY

sometimes
the biggest
and worst voice
is my own

I fill the air
with can-nots and will-nots
when all I want
is to be there.
but I am there
already

AMBIVALENCE

everything gets so
erratic, so chaotic
and loses form,
but only because we
make it so

security is an illusion
but so is uncertainty
we're so eager
to know everything
yet when knowledge
comes easily, it bores us

we want adventure
and a place to call home
a sense of identity,
but also opportunities
to reinvent ourselves,
to become someone
new every day

and as we get lost
busying ourselves with
what we think we want,
something interrupts us,
like a tap on the shoulder,
a reminder of what we
need in the most basic
and sensible way

AN UNDERSTANDING

you could learn
every language
in the world
but if someone
doesn't want to
understand you
then you don't
have to wait
for them to get
your message

ANGEL

are you an angel
sent to me from
heaven?
you've shown me
how to use my
eyes and ears
and thoughts again

you're the oil
that renews my
weathered skin
the water that
quenches and
heals my lips

out of nowhere
you arrived at
the doorstep of
my life, saving me
when I didn't think
I needed any saving,
giving me
companionship
when I thought
solitude was
the only way

ANXIETY

so scared
that your heart
might simply pop
like a little balloon

or maybe it will
implode, collapse
into itself like a
sinkhole

whatever the sensation,
it just won't stop as you
run out of comfort and
ground beneath your feet

ANYTHING

you can be
anything
if you can empathize
to the point
that you become
every thing.

ARMED

so much
of everything
in this place

no matter
how beautiful

somehow
can't escape
weaponization

ART

sometimes
it's necessary
to rebel
against the practical
by making use
of the beautiful

ASTOUND

she searches the waste
seemingly for nothing
but all she wants to do
is build something new.

you've got time,
you've got a lot of time,
so why not use it
to make this place
beautiful
like she does?

watch her use you
confuse you,
because you
are the material
and she makes you
into art
let her do her work
and she'll astound you.

ATTENTION

you're still trapped
so very trapped on
the outside, and what
they try to sell you
will pull you further in,
weigh you down
and distract you from
any true meaning
but in your mind
yes, in your mind
you are free.
remember that.
treasure that.

AUTOMATIC PEOPLE

automatic people
stop and cross
at the intersection
and do as they're told
when they hear yes
and when they hear no

BAD LAUGHTER

those who
laugh at you
are immature
even with themselves
not yet having developed
a proper coping mechanism
for their own innermost
fears

BANTER

calm
now,
calm.
don't you
see
it's just a
game they
play
so keep
your eyes
on the end
and your
ears
out of their
banter

BE ABLE

there are
plenty of reasons
why you can't,
if that's what
you want to see

but if you
open up and realize
your capability,
your capacity,
your aptitude,
a willingness
to be able

your able body,
and able mind,
and able spirit
will show you
that you can.

BEING HUMAN

wish I knew more
wish I weren't afraid
maybe I wouldn't
screw up
maybe I wouldn't
hurt others

BIG

do you know
how big you are?
I mean, really
do you know?

it's a question I mean to ask
sincerely
not a condescending
statement
about how tall
or wide
a human form
might be

have you ever
truly felt the amount of you
squeezed into this tiny,
temporary vessel?
you are immeasurable
and your strength
unquantifiable

and do you ever wonder
why people look down
at themselves
when they nearly leave?

it's because they finally see
how big they are
their souls reach into the sky
when they're no longer contained

so if anyone tries
to make you feel small,
remember just how big you are,
for you have more star-stuff
than there are stars
in the universe

and remind others
of how big they are,
that they, like you,
are indeed infinite
they are just contained
in this illusion,
this particular here,
this particular now,
to learn
to experience
to grow

BLOSSOM

do you breathe?
does your blood flow?
does your mind
know where your heart goes?

you are a blossom,
and my being cannot fathom
how you grow
and I know not
where you go
to sit and cry
when feeling low

you're a delicate fabric
whose tears I want to sew,
so let me gather your patches,
put you together
and make you glow

BOTH

he thought of her
as a vivid tattooed
piercing while
she found him
to be a beautifully
tragic bearded man

BOY

like when
a rooster
comes of age,
a boy is
no longer
a boy, but
a man
and becomes
king
of his own
destiny,
no longer
dictated
by others,
instead
standing on
his own

BRAND NEW

when you
came into this world
you arrived perfectly
shrink-wrapped,
a brand new model
ready to operate,
protected from
the elements

then your mother
gave you a bath
and got you ready
for all the
wear and tear
war and tar
weariness and tyranny
the well-being
and hell-being
of existence

so climb to the top
make your way
across the times
and find your way in,
the light of a million candles
waits patiently for you
to simply show up
as they look down
upon your face
to make sure you're
all right

BREAK

teeth clenched
everyone's got
their teeth clenched,
thumbs crossed,
muscles tight,
hearts galloping
as they try to keep up
with the orders,
with the screens,
and the machines

no amount of uppers
can keep your dog
ears alert forever
and no extra storage
will help you retain
the impossible amounts
of information you take in
just accept your humanity
and learn to take a break
before you break

BRIDGES

the bridge
is full of those
who say
let's get to
the castle

but the best
sight to see
is simply
watching
them.

BURST

anger floods him
like a massive downpour
onto the pavement.
he is a sponge
and gets so full
that he leaks and rains
down an acid
burning, dissolving
all it touches.
no one wrung him out.
his pores just took
on even more
until they burst.

CALCIFICATION

it's not hard
to get locked in
to simply stop

and stay seated
as our brains get
crusted over and
our insides corrode

so just like anything
else that's materialized
in this place, we must
keep ourselves up

always moving
always growing
always loving

CALL IT HOME

we don't need
to make a
living
we can just
make love
and call it
our home

CHAMELEON

thy
lifelong
enemy
constantly
blends
against
thee

CIVIL WAR

I'm not yours
at least that's what
your words seemed
to insinuate

how low do
we have to go
before stopping
the shutting out
of each other

CONSCIOUSNESS

pretty soon
the truth will be
revealed and all
the backwardness
that isn't seen,
but felt, will be
brought to
consciousness

yes, they will
get their day
and we will get ours
so let's not allow
ourselves to sink
down like them
just hold steady
and keep moving
towards the proper
destination

CONSISTENT

I wish
I could be
consistent
at everything I did

I would always feel
and do my best,
and everyday
I would
live to give
and live to love

but
even though
I try my best,
I don't always
feel or do
what is right
or good
or proper.

CONTROL

I am just a dream
or maybe a simulation
living in the space
of sleep
with a body
among bodies
on a plane,
some awkward
dimension,
a system
developed and promulgated
by someone else.
when will I wake
and realize
that I am the dreamer
instigating the dream?

CRAFT CURTAILED

I see everyone
contracting, shrinking,
turning inward, despite
their talents, despite
their gifts to the world

never have I seen
such beauty crumpled
up and tossed away
like a sauce-filled,
onion-laden
sandwich wrapper

when will you
be appreciated?
when will you
break out not as
a lone blister
on a battered foot,
but as a flower
in a compost pile

you'll be the first
sign of grace
and well-being,
reinvented out of
what might normally
be thrown out

DAYS

every day
is a brush on canvas
moving
leaving behind a trail
of fine lines
and sharp, abrupt edges

you are color
now fill in the gaps
bring in some life
share your humanness,
be the variable,
the one
which cannot be
lived without

DAYS IN AUTUMN

my mind's a mess
and I'm excited
to see you
and I can't wait
to get out of here
because all I can
think about is
running out to you
on a sunny day

DETERMINATION

in a time
when nearly all
inconveniences
have been conquered
it's still difficult
to dominate the will,
because so much
has been done
to manipulate it,
in order to make us forget
that it belongs to us.

DISCERNMENT

sometimes
I wish that
discerning
between
good and bad
could be easy
like in the movies

but sometimes
your enemy
isn't out
to get you,
they're simply
discontented
or ill-informed

DISCORD

oh how it fills my lungs
and disrupts my breathing,
the air you expel
that some may call words,
but what I simply name
contagion

your sounds are entities
that take form and spread
on their own
contaminating my being
latching on to my outsides
like ivy, choking me
draining me of life
until I fall,
a dry and hollow branch,
to be eaten by things
that roam the depths
of the earth

sometimes I wonder
if the only way
to salvage myself
is to simply cut away
from the very ones
I thought were
helping

DOWN

it sets in
like a fog
a heavy screen
that can't be lifted
you hesitate to move forward
since you fear what's ahead
so you stay stuck
because the only safe places
are down and back

DREAMER, HEALER

he is a healer
and seeker of truth
the kindling to a flame
most incredible
and unstoppable,
the pebble which starts
an avalanche, the current
that wears away at
barriers and conventions

they laugh at him
try to throw him
off his game
and compress his dreams
into small, ridiculous things
and they expect an apology
for who he is and the purpose
for which he was born

DRIVE EAST

I dearly want
to travel all
the way east
and though I know
I could just fly there,
what I really wish for
is that it would
simply take forever

it doesn't need to be
agonizing or painful,
after all, I can be patient.
it's just that I want to
soak in every detail,
every dry throat through
the desert, every pothole
in the half-done roads,
every break down
and push start

I want the details,
not in writing,
not on film
or in talk,
but up close and
personal, through
my own eyes,
and lungs and ears,
touched by my
own hands

EAGLES

if you think
that you
can't
you might
want to check
the people
with whom you
surround
yourself

ECCENTRIC

lonesome
yet eccentric
clumsy
yet calculated

you live
your life
like an episode
of Mr. Bean

clever and innocent
wisdom abounding
a confused
and quiet soul

ELECTRON PROMISES

jealousy
come sail the sea
spend your days
in the maze
fall asleep
in silent sleet
till summer talks
past beating clocks
spring awake
on beds of straw
tell of dreams
and what you saw
find the feeling
full of pain
know that clouds
don't always rain
place the sun
upon your mind
leave it somewhere
you can find
all the thoughts
they take you here
and keep you out
of structured fear

EUROPEAN CITIES

old towns
with decades of mystery
foundations crumble
yet continue to be
built upon
but we all know
they could never truly
hide all their scars,
those subtle carved impressions
brought on by generations
of fighting and struggling

EVERYBODY

everybody's right
everybody wants to be
everybody knows
everybody wants to know

everybody lacks
because they want to have
everybody blames
but nobody owns the blame
everybody's scared
even though they look tough

everybody loves
everybody wants to
everybody's loved
everybody wants to be loved

EXIST

to exist
is to grow
and change
continually

whether gradually
or hastily
this goes beyond
time and space

so perhaps
infinity is defined
as simply
persisting

EXPERIENCE YOU

we've written many
letters back and forth
and though you've
told me everything
there are still things
I'd like to know
do you crash and rush
like the waves of the sea?
or do you bend like
branches in the wind?
is your voice
a lion's roar?
or do you whisper
like a cool summer breeze?
are your hands
as tender as a day off
or as soft as silken sheets?
however you may be
I want to be there
I want to experience you

FAR FROM TYPICAL

staring into space
what a lovely face
see you in the mirror
only getting clearer
you age yourself
to portray yourself
and act a part
to make it art
stay original
far from typical
experience you
to find what's true

FEAR'S INFLUENCE

it's no longer
a matter of
good or bad,
the days of
such simplicity
are over

instead, you will
be judged by
how much you
let fear influence
your actions

FEEL

those
who are sensitive
are the eyes
and ears among us,
they are truly human
as they remind us
how to feel
in a world that
teaches us not to

FEST

you took me to a place
where the girls wore
those old dresses
all colored up
just like the lights
lining the tents
and the Ferris wheel
how I wish I had the courage
to ask for a dance
or pay for a drink
at the bar which
they built on a carousel
to dizzy the dizzied
and get them
to buy another,
tricking them into
thinking they'll
see straight

FILL YOUR HEART

I'm going to
fill your heart
like a book
but instead
of mere words
I'll give you
my love.

FIND

you went away to find yourself
and haven't been home in years
they sit and wait for you to phone
but barely break before you return

what could they
want from you
and you from them?
the past is calling you
to make your plans
for the future now

and you'll make things happen
and they'll happen for you
even halfway across the world
even halfway across the sun

FIRST SNOW

first snow
always brings
a certain calm
demeanor
perfect
for putting
the year into
review
as all goes
quiet
on the newly
decorated
landscape

FOAM

if you
had it all
you'd be a
bathing wasp,
soaking in the
sweet, sweet milk
of a half-consumed
cappuccino

FOOL

I don't care
what you were
to your country
but to me
you are a traitor

perhaps you were
a lawful son
with a gun
but not that way
with yours

when it's all
against one
there's room
for only one
fool
the one who's
different
regardless of if
he's righteous,
self-righteous
or mad

learn that
it's such a
game
and that
you are
the fool

FOR LIVING

cells were
meant to grow
so let them.
bodies were
made to move
so dance.
minds were
set to be free
so free them.
eyes were
created for sight
so uncover them.
ears are
for hearing
so listen.
lives are
for living
so live them.

FORGOTTEN

what causes us
to put up walls
and be so afraid?
is it a denial
of our nature?
or a rejection
of the notion
that we are all
human beings?

sometimes
we are so awful
to each other
and instill fear
as a poor attempt
to cover pain
because we've forgotten
happiness
and lost touch
with peace.

FRANTIC FLY

frantically
moving about
the room
in odd
figure eights,
while unbeknownst
to him,
a window
is open
the entire
time.

FREE

you belong
to nowhere
and to no one
it's not
an insult because
you're unique
you're free

FUNCTIONING

they held him back
yes they held him down
pressing on his shoulders
putting weight on his feet

I'm not tired, I'm not lazy

and others simply wondered
why he wasn't getting up
why he wasn't joining
the other functioning,
social wind-up
talking machines

GHOST

ghost in the window
shocking others
but haunted in and of
yourself

you just want to see
the light of day
as you envy
the playing children

they too will grow up
while you grow weary
and remain confined
to the walls
which you could
so easily permeate

GIANT ORCHESTRA

I am just a beat
in a song that never ends
and I wait, like an actor backstage,
to play my small, but necessary role,
anticipating the one right line
to speak,
the one right note
to strike,
simultaneously significant
and modestly minuscule,
because I alone am not the tune,
and neither are you.
together
we orchestrate ourselves
to create the sounds
of space.

GOLD

I'd rather
spend my time
searching the world
for gold
than staying here
trading silver

GRAVITY

let it all
fall away
the very things
that brought you here
come back to Earth

fear not
because you're already
in space and gravity
no longer holds
you captive

GROWTH

this growth
has gotten you
tired of simply
feeling full,
because you're
finally ready
to be nourished
and healed
and if you're
scared, don't be
because the confusion
and lack of direction
will soon pass.

HER HOMELAND

I want to breathe
my own air and set
foot on the ground
which my ancestors
plotted and paved

I want to feel
that bustle and rush,
the orderly disorder
the closeness of
community

it may be loud,
it may be pushy
you might feel
hurried, but it is
my home

HOME

can't find
a way to fit
even when I act
like I don't

wish I could
feel at home
even away from home
better yet at home

HOW TO LOVE

I wish
you knew
how to love
you could
love me more
I wish
I knew
how to love
I could love
you and me
more.

HURT WALLS

why do we
bark at each other
like a bunch of
hurt animals
pretending we're
the only ones
experiencing pain?

there's just so much
misunderstanding
in this place
and no time to
clear things up
and the feelings just
get too strong,
they create a pride
that's capable of
building high walls.

IDEAL

there may never be
an ideal moment,
but there is a time
for every thing

there may never be
a perfect situation,
but some are much
easier than others

there may never be
the right people,
but cherish those
who stand by you

IF WE COULD

if we could be happy
from the inside out
we would have enough
to give to each other

if we could conquer
the fear of ourselves
we would dump fabrication
and have real conversations

if we could feel
sufficiently understood
we would listen with
the intent to understand

if we could see
our similarities
we might realize how
much division we create

if we could reach out
in kindness, not hatred
we might have friends
and no longer be lonely

ILLUMINATED

I've never felt
so clean
so wanted
so loved
and surrounded
by an illuminated
embrace.

you absorb me
inclusively
and I choose you.
do not cry
do not cry anymore
because I am with you
I am a part of you
I am you.

IMAGINATION

imagination
starts to leak
drop by drop
and eventually
spills as if
blindly beaten
out of a piñata

we grow up,
if that's the
acceptable term,
but the child inside
is still curious
though forced
to sit still

shaky legs,
sleepless nights,
and a wandering heart
are signs of your
unused energy,
your unfulfilled
potential

let age
be an integer
not a determinant
of whether you
remain trapped
within a system.
or create your own.

IMPOSSIBLE, IMAGINED

the expression
on your face
seems as though
I told you I'd build
a bridge to the sun
impossible!
your rolling eyes assert
doubtful at best!
your pursed lips reveal

but I will show you
yes, I will show you
that there is nothing
impossible or imagined
about this place
and you will see
yes, you will see
that there is nothing
impossible or imagined

IMPRESS

was there ever
a time when things
were less "in-your-face?"
when did it become
a requirement
to always be so "driven,"
to constantly have
such a caffeinated enthusiasm?
who told us to act this way
in order to get a job, to get by?

if you want to know about me
just ask. my resume
won't tell you who I am
or what role I play,
which is almost always
myself.

not calling you fake,
but you won't get
what you want to hear,
you won't be falsely impressed

you should know
I'm not after the biggest house
or newest car. no.
instead, I seek the root
of what makes us whole,
and I'm not about
to reset my bearings
and go off course.

IMPRINT

though your chapters
may already be finished
you are the editor
and you can change
how the rest
of the scenes
play out
before they are
printed

IMPROVISE

I can't blame you
for being practical
or at least wanting
me to be.

I just find it funny
because I think
I caught the creative bug
from you.

your job was to
improvise and overcome.
when will you see that
I'm doing the same?

IN MOTION

hey!
it's not just for horses.
I say it because I'm alive.

yes, my heart is beating
and my eyes are blinking
while my lungs soak up
the sweet air

my muscles prepare to
tense and twitch and relax
to perform one controlled
fall after another

I am moving
and whether this motion
is supposed to be controlled
by someone or something else
is now out of the question

because you gave me
brains to think
and senses to feel
and a conscience to heal.

universe,
let me be a world
within your world.

Joseph Michael Lowery

INDUSTRIALIZATION

industry arrived
and the people
became as false
and disconnected
and store-bought
as the goods
they consumed

INNER SPACE

now that all additives
have been removed
you can appreciate
your own energy,
no longer hopped up
in order to keep up,
because the natural
human state is
calm and inquisitive,
not needing to fight
or feed on adrenaline.

INTENTIONS

sweep me up
like particles of dust
on a restaurant's
dirty floor at closing
and I'll pour into you
my purest intentions,
the highest grade of oil
I can offer for your fryers

INTERRUPTIONS

smiles and waves
are precursors to
their half-hearted,
empty exchanges
don't they see me?
they ask themselves
don't they want
to know me?
each one wants
to be known
even to himself
so much that he
doesn't even leave
room to hear
another's story.

INTIMIDATION

intimidation
is just a front
for weakness

truth
hides not
and to the weak
it can appear
intimidating

INVADE

you
invade me
like the rising milk
in an unstirred
coffee

JOIN THE RANKS

it's okay
sometimes
to disappear
there are days
which call you
into the background
to fall out
of the march
to develop
your own steps
those who wrongly
accuse you of
hiding are simply
curious, always
wanting information,
desperately needing
status updates
and further intelligence
but do not mistake
this for what they
might call it.
this is not laziness.
this is not depression.
this is not coldness.
and once you
join the ranks
again they will
greet you and
they will notice
the change
immediately

JUST TIME

you'll get
everything
but it might
not arrive
at the time
you expect
or in the
right order

LATE NIGHTS

what do you seek
late at night?
the ideas are growing,
further blooming from
the seed, within the
bulbous form atop
your shoulders

you want more
you wait for the time
you'll surpass them,
you wait until
you can prove them
wrong, but you already
do every passing day

LATE UNDERSTANDING

you will
never
understand me
not in
a million
years
and I will
never
understand you
and I won't
even try
for another
two million

LAUGHING IN THE RAIN

I laughed
in the rain
no longer caring
as I soaked it up
and let it
wash through me

and when
the storm had cleared
all that polluted
my waters
trickled away
and I was clean.

LAUGHTER

wholehearted laughter
keeps you young
while easing the pains
of constant growth,
making each day
more bearable
than the last

find a reason to laugh
make room within every
second to smile
your face and body
know how to relax,
how to let go,
so be as you are
and don't forget.

LEARNING TO TALK

it's contagious
and fills the crater
I don't have to act or plead
it just pours through
and becomes the new me.

I watch it change me,
and change others.
we wear our pronunciations
like new shirts,
all different colors
all bright and new
and vivid

we're all cotton
we glow, we fade
we get dirty
and then washed again
we break but can be mended
if we're not thrown away.

LET GO

one achieves wisdom
when he lets go
of his need to be right
and when he is willing
to admit to his mistakes,
for he is human
and truth, objective

LET THE RAIN

let the rain
soak through your hair
and seep into your soul
let it cleanse the contaminants
that make you forget
who you really are

LIGHTER

their unhappiness,
their lead-weight
attitudes
hold you down

at first they put weight
on your head,
so it hung down
and brought your neck
forward,
then your back
and you could no longer
stand straight.
now it almost crushes
you completely,
as you can't even lift yourself
out of bed.

have you forgotten?
this weight is not yours.
it belongs to someone else.
now tell me,
do you feel lighter?
rise again.

LIGHTS AND STARS

dear
I hope
to present you
with my greatest
ideas
and transmit to you
what the stars emit,
all that I soak up
but cannot soak up anymore.

spaces
get filled so frequently now
so I must give,
as it's my only connection
to the ground,
otherwise I will dream
into the lights
honing in on what they
give off

LIKE YOU DO

scared
perhaps too many
want what you want
choosing what you choose
but they don't do it
not the way you do
and they don't want it
like you want it.

LIVING THE BEAT

today I woke
to a rhythm
that may not
feel my own,
but somehow
is my own,
and though it
didn't seem to
take any grand
effort to complete
my given tasks
this fire became
the locomotive
that started to pull
everything along

Joseph Michael Lowery

LONGER DAYS

daylight stays
longer
and the sun comes
sooner
it becomes easier
to wake up.

the energy
of a new year
fills the spirit
with fresh air
and eagerly pumping
blood.

let it
rise
let it
circulate
let it
contaminate
the rest.

LUCK

sometimes
luck flows
when you really need it
just when you think
you've completely run out
there will be more and more
just enough to keep you going

even when you reach
the point of falling,
something or someone out there
wants to keep you afloat
wants you to stand tall
wants to teach you
that fear is just
an illusion

its only purpose
is to show us
how to believe
in our abilities
and that temporary struggle
makes for a sweeter reward
in due time

LYING WHITE HAIRS

those lying
white hairs
lying on your head,
they start
to take it over,
lying about your
outer age

what you've always
done merited that,
and it left you
worried about keeping up,
having and being
enough

but you always were
enough
and you never
actually needed
that genius fiction

MACHINE

you are
an automated
machine
but not
in a way
that you'd like

stop saying
yes
when you mean
no

because
it's a selfish
and self-destructive
act,
this people-pleasing
addiction

MEASURE

shining sun
and golden sky
all is good
that meets the eye
see the forest
on a hill
as we drive by
yet sit so still

hold this moment
for a bit
hold it now
before it quits

because one day
we will let go
of things that pull us
to and fro
and every minute
will be measured
by if it was
or was not treasured

MENSCH

hier
bin ich kein mensch
sondern
dein produktionsmodus

METALLIC

young, flowing, metallic
you'll never truly know
until you've reached
madness and made it
back, until you've
realized you've lived
your whole life
and it's built up
into this moment.

MIND, MOUTH, HEART

calm
intense
not intended
to intimidate
not meant
to misconstrue
these eyes
won't judge
this heart
won't hurt
this mouth
won't curse
this mind
won't conspire

MORNING GRATITUDE

how good it feels
to finally wake
and sense this
confirmation

drive into the day
the meaning
you've been waiting
all night to express

tend to all
that surrounds you
with love and
thankfulness

MOVE

always moving
sometimes rushing
mostly chasing
kept alive by
what moves me

MY MOMENT

this is my moment
it's not about you
it's not about them
and I've got the radio on
and the volume up
and my song came on
and when it's done,
when the car's stopped
I'll open the flood gates
once again
but until then
this is my moment
and no one can
take it away

MY SHADOW

I try to understand
I try to get along
yet how do I trust
when I don't see
the same in return,
when your methods
are at odds with mine,
and your whole livelihood
is at war with me
when I have no war
to wage?

you defend yourself,
but against what
and from whom?
you act as if
my breath alone
is enough to intimidate
but all I do is exist,
and for that I can't
be sorry.

NAVIGATE

I get up with the sun
and stay lit with the moon
there's just so much life
to live
and so many ways
to roam

sleep cannot keep
me from enjoying
the spectacular sights
that arise day and night

paint a house
paint the sky
paint the mind

each moment is an imprint,
a new groove to be played
by the needle in later decades
an ornament of remembrance,
a star by which to navigate.

NEW LENS

no room
for guilt
no energy
for false assumptions
no time
to make judgements
unaffected
by the extreme
highs and lows
that invade reality
as the picture
comes into focus
under a new lens

NEW WINGS

you don't
have to tell
everyone
what you're doing

fly low
until you're ready
to show off
your new wings

NIGHT SKY

night sky
window to the moon
bright-bulbed companions
shine over me and you
doing little light shows
provided that the space
grows big enough to serve
their ever-glowing grace

NOISE

for years
you made noise
but truly hadn't
anything to say

then suddenly
there were too many
messages and a certain
vivacity to your
thoughts

they arrived
on pages upon pages
as a certain inner unrest,
and the energetic bee
which rumbled in your heart
left behind a trail of fire

it desperately wanted to escape,
not out of anger or utter madness,
but rather because
its eagerness to be of use
couldn't be contained
in a vessel
so small

NOTHING HIDES

when you start
to see things
you haven't seen before
it means you're
paying attention
you've become present
and nothing can
hide from you

OBJECTIVE

there are moments
when things are so
effortlessly coordinated
and organized

you can't be stopped,
all distractions
are pushed aside,
things that held you back
can no longer

now the larger framework
is in view,
perhaps there are
no longer frames,
everything can be seen,
neither intense nor mild

OBLIGATION

I don't know
if I'll ever
come to an
understanding
with the
differences
of others

for now,
I'm happy
that there
is no
obligation
to do so.

OBSERVER

looking out
into endless blue
where water meets sky
the wind gently
brushes my face
and sun heats my back
giving life to my frame.

boats, slightly tilted
propel across
the sparkling bed
of cerulean diamonds
with full sheets
catching my eyes
calming my breath

I used to dream
of being here
finally unchained
no longer ordered about
by the waves
and becoming both
observer and overseer

OCEANS

chaotic waves
and calm seas
dark days
and light breeze

sometimes you
almost sink
other times
you start to think

what would the ocean
and land be like
if they stood still
and didn't fight?

would they still
shape each other?
would they hide
in the art of cover?

though at times extreme
whether by chance,
or perhaps foreseen,
twists turn to dance

changes force upon us
the need to adapt,
to readily flow
to prevent collapse

the treasure exists
in neither up nor down
because the energy of both
is what brings you around

let yourself be driven
from side to side
but remember to push back
and enjoy the ride

because you and this world
and everything in it
are alive and in motion
and exist without limit

OLD MYSTERIES

at this moment
I watch my life
eat itself away
quicker each day,
as the sand leaks out
faster now
to the bottom.

I ponder and seek
so many things,
they can't even
begin to be conquered

and I get so cynical
because there is so much
more than here.
what is a curious soul to do,
wait another lifetime?
I wish I were clever enough
to answer this myself,
to ease my own
excitement and anticipation.

when will all be revealed,
I wonder,
in full color?
for now only questions
answer questions
attempting to keep
old mysteries at bay.

OLD TOWN

they cleaned up
and built over
everything from the past
just to make others forget
the years of struggle
and tragedy and
times which spawned
bravery and cowardice,
righteousness and sin,
only to be forgotten
except by those whose
souls stayed trapped

ONE LAST LIFE

I want sleep
I want home
I want bliss
I want comfort
one last push
one last round
one last effort
one last life

meant for you
but not for you
meant for you
but not for you
one last push
one last round
one last effort
in this last life

Joseph Michael Lowery

OUR DEVICES

these electronics
won't leave me alone
they're always badgering,
hounding me for attention
and I wonder if there's even
a human being on the
other end of this tin can

but as I attempt to
contemplate such an idea
another beep, another buzz
and—where was I again?
time to pay attention
to the all-seeing,
all-listening and
all-knowing
device

OUT OF THE PEN

this sort of life
we've created
tends to break us.
why do we continue
to hold it up?
why do we deride
those who
step out and try
to fix it?

OUTSIDE

what do you see
when you look outside?
are there trees
and roads and buildings
or is there a way out?
gazing through that
promising window
you see an escape
to something better
and now you are out there
not bothering to look
at all the frustration
and all the nothingness
they made you feel
when you were
still inside

OVERNIGHT SUCCESS

I'm convinced
that overnight success
doesn't exist,
rather it grows
each day
from a little seedling,
sprouting and forming

every moment
it rearranges itself
until it finally
grows so immense
that no one can help
but acknowledge
its presence

it then continues
to flourish
over many days
and many nights,
otherwise it will
die out
before anyone
even discovers
its existence.

PAPER PLANES

this is the way
that I manage
the chaos in my brain
the thoughts
they take flight
but on paper
they have a place
to land and be
guided home

PARTNER

you are my friend
you are the one
I tell you my secrets
I give you my love
in good times or bad
when happy or sad
I confide in your goodness
and the days we've had
in sickness and health
you've been by my side
scarceness and wealth
leave you nothing to hide
so take my hand
I'll keep holding on
we'll keep chasing sunsets
until we are gone

PATTERNS

lives end up sad
due to misunderstandings,
holding on to pain,
and living out the same
misidentified patterns
day after day

PEN AND PAPER

where do all
your thoughts lead?
you write those words
not just to fill up space
but instead wish to
paint with words
and translate thoughts
into light, color, and sound
because after all
why should a page
be so plain?

PERCEPTIONS

nothing
is what it seems
many
of the perceptions
will
sooner or later
be
turned on their heads
because
anything is possible

PERMANENCE

you are such
a concept and
the more I think
and hope and pray
about you
the more I forget
that you're just
a person like me
whose imagination
carries you away
grasping desperately
for things as fleeting
as a single breath,
wishing them to be
permanent

PLACE

you have
no home
but only
because
you never
completely
belonged
to a single
place

PLAYGROUND

children laugh and ride
while mothers watch
with eagle eyes
they hide and play
the day away
while their elders dream
of younger times
when every day
was an adventure
and every experience
brand new

PLEASURE BOMB

it's an escape
that takes you far away
just to intensify
and highlight
your senses
for a short
clip of the present

it's an explosion
then an outage,
mere distortion
of the moment
providing constant
weakness
a wanting
a hunger
a lack

it's a calculus limit
perpetually approaching
but obsessively keeping
you on the cusp
and as you get closer
you never actually reach
the destination

PRESSURE PEOPLE

jobs are
occupied by
people who
might call
themselves
confrontational
but in reality,
they can't even
face themselves

PROCESS

when will you
realize that you
aren't truly free
until you stop being
someone else's process?

PROPER GREETING

you
come at me
like you're
about to
leave me
decapitated
when all I want
is for you to
have a nice day
what do you want
me to learn
that you haven't?

QUESTIONS

are we cruel
or do we to try
to justify our pain?
are we hurtful
or do we lack
in understanding?
are we judging
or afraid of
getting to know
the unknown?

QUIET MOMENT

quiet moments
have gone
from a leisurely
surplus
to a reclusive
rarity
as nearly
everything
attempts to
trample on your
attention

RAIN AND INK

the rain
flows like
the ink
from my pen,
lightly
and
naturally,
not causing
the slightest
disturbance,
only effortlessly
painting,
paving,
shaping.

RATIONALIZE

how can I rationalize
any lack of distrust
in those irrational eyes?
I have tried and tried
to pretend to realize
that in your actions
there were no lies
I'd like to
find you ethical
at least with others
even if I am
the only exception
so in rationalizing
I hope you see
I wish nothing
but the best
and I don't want
to harm you

REARRANGE

can't get
my head around
what will make
it work

all this
rearranging
and shifting
is a nocturnal
game of Tetris
an eternal
puzzle

and I'm watching
and waiting
for all the
pieces to come
together.

Joseph Michael Lowery

RESILIENCE

this is a visual record
of your wrinkles
and how they progress.
like your heart,
your skin gets harder,
and the lines deeper
and more pronounced.

why should this happen?
God just wanted you to learn.
like exercise and boot camp
break down muscles and men
you are resilient
and come back stronger
and smarter each time.

RESISTANCE

resistance
is what makes
things difficult.
you try to force something
to fit and it won't
you hope everyday
that someone will quit
and they don't.

how much stress,
how much tension,
has to build
before we get sick,
before we finally break?

we don't need
to take everything in,
but we can at least
be conscious about
how much energy
goes into being
against something

how much time is wasted
by putting the brakes on
something that wants to
stay in motion,
when in reality,
it can be slowed
and then placed
in a new direction?

REVERSE, REVERSE!

I've got those
reversing goggles
and I didn't have to
pay for them
and no, I didn't
steal them, either
all I had to do
was leave home
to a place where
everything is opposite
and upside down
compared to how it's
supposed to be
all is inverted
those who seem
trustworthy aren't
to be trusted
and those who are
successful
are only slightly
more than boring,
and this new context
around me seems to
change my role in
the world—the eternal loser
pretty soon, they'll be
throwing tomatoes at me
but I know who I am
even if I'm the only one
even if everything gets all
blurred and distorted

RIGHT

I won't
stop
and I won't
make excuses
or try to
explain myself
for what I
believe to be
right and true

RISE

time to rise
time to move
if you are
who you say
you are
then do it
if you are
who you think
you are
then be it
the morning
is waiting for
you to show
your greatness
act it out
live it out

ROLES

the fear
of not having enough
buying
into the scarcity lie
is what turns us into
drones

it makes us think
we need to do things,
which creates a reality
where we are poorer
not only in material,
but also in spirit,
love, and satisfaction

open
the door to being
human
be who you always were
and stop playing
roles

SAME RISK

wouldn't it be
easier just to stay
bundled up in bed?
the cold morning air
seems so threatening
on days like these,
which are becoming
ever more frequent

life seems too risky
in the outer world,
another quirky idea
you picked up after
getting hurt, a kind of
mental flu or gentle fluke
that came and hit you
when you were already down

stay the same,
you hear off in the
distance somewhere
stay comfortable,
as this irrational fog
cloaks you from hat to shoe,
but your real self pleads
to be heard, as it speaks
what is true

Joseph Michael Lowery

SAND

what is eating away
at your flesh
and shrinking your bones?
you thought you were the fire.
are you now being consumed by it?

it's such a virus,
such a sorry misunderstanding
stealing your youth
degrading your clock

things get less memorable
as the sand passes through
the narrow tunnel
until the vessel drops.

SAY IT NOW

please excuse
this sudden
surge of words,
though they seem
to arise out of
nowhere

I've actually
been saving
them up, waiting
not avoiding,
timing and calibrating,
planning and reworking

yes, sometimes I'm
a perfectionist
though you'd never
guess it
but I always know
when the right time
comes to say
what must be spoken

SEE YOU

I'll see you again
I'll see you again
because you're not
that far

I'll see you again
I'll see you again
because you live
in my heart

I'll see you again
I'll see you again
no matter where
you are

I'll see you again
I'll see you again
you beautiful work
of art

SELF-MUTILATION

it's just so much
easier to pick apart
at yourself while pretending
it's going to fill another hole
created by the same
bad habit—one mistake
for self-preservation,
for self-beautification,
but it's only marred this
perfect shiny slate
that you were given
you can't even
argue about it
being an engraving
or impressive piece
of abstract art.
when all is said and done
it's just dirty, scuffed
and scathed, and you
try to hold it up
or put out or exist
or whatever it is you do
but you just can't
keep running without
all cylinders working
properly

SERIAL

quiet smiling eyes
bottled up about to burst
dangerous being

SEVERE PROCRASTINATION

this is an
emergency
and the only
way I can get
this off my back
is if I treat it with
the correct amount
of urgency

SITUATIONS

some situations
test our limits
they make us feel
uncomfortable
they make us grow
tougher skin

slight callouses
allow us to handle
rough things

we have the choice
to still feel
and grow stronger
or to grow numb
and attempt avoiding
further pain

SLEEPING IN

even if it were
your job to
wake up the
entire world,
not everyone
would rise at
the same time
so let the
long sleepers
sleep
let their ideas
incubate until
they are ready
to bloom

START TO FINISH

a friend said
you're losing time
that way.

he referred to
wishing our days away
before they'd even
had a chance
to begin.

your days leave you
little by little
so fill your time
with things that
you can't wait
to start
and don't want
to end.

STILL THERE

I haven't gone away,
not completely,
I'm just moving on,
I tried, but it's been
quite enough
at least for now

maybe we can
attempt this
again later,
when your blaming,
taming, defaming
voice gets out
of my head, because
it's interrupting my
processes

and this teeming,
reeling feeling
is quite demeaning
constantly repeating,
mistreating, attacking
ransacking the depths
of my heart

I thought there were still
secret reserves of love,
hidden safely away,
but they've now
been depleted

STRAWS

I've finally come
to a realization
and my disdain for it,
my distaste for it
has got me undone

I feel myself
becoming so small
and powerless, while
they quench their thirst
slurping me up,
as if through straws

pretty soon
my own glass
will be empty,
and now I know
why they smile

they laugh
ever so freely
at my foolishness
as I gave my time,
my efforts, all too
willingly

no more
you won't dry me up
even if you tried
snorting me through
paper currency

SUCCESS

freedom
is knowing
you can do anything

happiness
is knowing
what you want

success
is identifying both
with a humble sense
of gratitude

SUPERNOVA

your spirit
glows like
a dying star

your giant calm
and wise radiance
shine out of
a most pure love

SURREAL

everything is so
surreal all along
the track and field
everyone's strange
everyone's not ok
yet we're all fine

the stadium is full
and so is the grass
of red uniforms
of cheering
of adrenaline

it all passes
from season
to season
as do we
into the world
out on our own

SWIM

I'd like to swim
through the colors
of a fog

the air would be so thick
it would make me light
I'd simply take flight

but I wouldn't choke or drown
it would just pass through
and propel me

SYNCHRONIZE

surrender
and if you don't
like the word,
synchronize

get in time
find your place
in infinite space
conduct your own
orchestra

be receptive
and observe
as things
fall in line
orderly
but naturally

TALKS

words to a feeling
like evidence to a crime
always around
but sometimes hard to find
speak your mind
if you know what to say
talk for years
about one single day

THE COMMUTE

a shiver runs
up her spine
and it's neither
pain nor fear
nor pleasure

it's just the
sharp and frigid,
clear early morning
jolting her awake
as she takes
her first step
outside

she's carrying
the dark, shouldering
the stars
and is the one
who sees to it
that the day
begins

THE NEED

why do things get
chaotic
for you?
how much of that
chaos
do you choose
just to feel
alive?

Joseph Michael Lowery

THE SPACE OF NOW

what do you do
when you get so high?
you just can't contain
the length of the sky
every thought floats
just like a bird
because nothing here
is too absurd.

you start to dive deep
but not into sadness
since so much paint
can't be put onto canvas
build a fire out of a droplet
pull a button
out of a pocket
dance in time
and make a pattern
send good vibes
out to Saturn

climb the mountain
to the Dalai Lama
and re-enact
the earliest drama
because your history
will be played back in song
and you'll return
before not too long
so live the moment
like a holy cow
because it's all happening
and it's happening now.

THE VARIABLE

you just
got so good
at sitting,
at taking in
information
piece by piece
and not doing
anything with it

you never
imagined
you'd be this
sitting stone
the antithesis
of human
slowly eroding
losing your
conglomerates
numbing and dumbing
all feeling

hiding the fact
that you, too,
have a soul,
have a mind,
and are meant
to move and
interact and
have influence
and are capable
of being inspired

you are not the
mere observer,
you are the actor
you are the variable
and without you,
everything changes

THE WATCHER

I am not this
I am just watching
and as I experience
this fleeting moment,
simultaneously important
yet unimportant in the
grand scheme of things,
I am like the dot in a line
one star in a sky full of them
a grain of sand on the beach,
and like these, I will soon enough
be smudged away, collapse inward
and get washed out into the ocean.

THE WIN

let's work together
let's aim for the real win,
not the one in which
one profits
and the other pales

I mean the kind of win
in which we challenge
each other to the end
in order to achieve
something greater
than one could achieve alone
because if only
one of us wins
then we all lose

we are here
to elevate one another
to pass the test together
as we, by design
have complimentary roles

THRIVE

did you thrive?
were you alive?
somehow, somewhere
you got a little lost
in the loneliness
in the stress
in others

these days
you're spent
a dimly glowing star
losing light
fading into space
burning fuel
feeding the illusion

when you leave
you'll be the grand finale,
an explosion of lights,
and every particle
every speck of dust
will extend to the edge
of the cosmos.

TRAINS

rattling the tracks
doors open wide, people flow
the exchange takes place

the gray seats await
the warmth of new company
sifting through the aisles

stillness starts to move
colors pass the windows by
buildings become fields

the talking starts now
quiet, nice, unimportant
a moment of calm

an announcement comes
time to rise as motion slows
touch ground, on your way

TRAVELER, WANDERER

you are
the traveler
you are
the wanderer
lay your bags
down
and let your
heart
find home.

TREES SLEEP

trees sleep barren while
the leaves land colorfully
scattered on a hill

TRULY RESTED

I want to sit
in silence
and blend into
the darkness,
total rest as
it would be

not a violent act
or a selfish one,
just a break from
the noise, the movement,
from that invisible
push on your shoulders,
the tugging at your heart

eyes need not close
nor must lungs stop
their respiration

blood can still
circulate but
mind need not navigate

because I'm
full as it is
and would
like to spend time
being nothing

TURN

turn me
around
pick me up
and flip me
upside down
with your eyes
that's what you do
because your mind
doesn't want to see
me the way I really am

UNAFRAID

you build the future
while they build doubt
you always change
while they never will

UNKNOWN POTENTIAL

you were given
the gift of
being surrounded
by disciplinarians
and though you
mistook their being,
their behavior,
for harshness,
you only wish
you saw the
greatness they
saw in you.
they knew the
secret, that talent
left undeveloped
would only sit and
fester, as opposed
to what it was meant
to do, which is to grow
and inspire others
and to add to
the countless examples
of what human beings
can do

US

people like us don't
space out like
others think we do
we just talk to stars.

VITAL

life is a pleasure
and full of pressure
life is a present
and begs for your presence
fill it with good
and live like you should
don't wish it away
or you'll be on your way
to filling a desk
having wasted your breath

WAITING ROOM

waiting
in a bland government
hallway
you hope you have
your papers
don't forget
your papers
did they even give you
the right papers?

and when they see you
you plead for a chance,
fumbling your words
trying to say them
the right way.

all the truck rides
and ferries
and miles walked
and run
the adrenaline
the rain
the heat
have amounted to this
day of waiting
day of hoping
day of worry.

WAR IS THE MEDIUM

violence
during "peacetime"
scares some
to make others
look powerful

WAYPOINTS

who says
that dreams
are for sleep?
what if they are
outlines of goals,
waypoints
to guide you home?
and all those obstacles,
all those people
and things and situations,
what if they are mirages?

WHEN

when will we awaken
to the full color spectrum
that is, the world
which surrounds us?

when will the hairs
on our arms start to stand,
even when the sun is out,
not because it's cold,
but rather because
we acknowledge and are thankful
for our own consciousness?

when will we realize
that our days have
given us plenty,
even in ways
we might not understand?

when will we stop
asking what we can get
out of life and start
adding to it,
making this existence better,
not only for us, but for others?

'when' is the question
and we can leave it
unanswered, if we want,
or we can realize that now
is the appropriate time

WHO BURIED LOVE?

I am love
I'm not here
to tell you
how to do it.
instead, I will reveal
what is already in you,
just by pointing at it,
just by tapping your shoulder
and reminding you of it.

you are peace
and I learn from your example
and it sticks to me,
the contagion of harmony,
a sample of what
this place could be,
or better yet,
what it already is
by its very nature.

when did kindness
get masked by complication?
when did we get distracted
from the simple, universal truths
that aid in our well-being?
when did we turn against each other,
lose our connectedness,
out of fear and lack
of proper communication?

days like today
call for us to let go
of things that place themselves
on top
while pushing
the most important matters
to the bottom
of the landfill.

WHOLE

you are whole
and not lacking
you are everything
in one
all that is necessary
exists within

there is no need
to look outside and take.
instead let out
what you already have

share it with others
and uncover
what also exists
within them

WINTER MORNING

a warm cup
takes the bite out
of a cold winter morning
and a bite
warms the heart
and oils the gears
for the day to come
a short silence
before the chaos
continues

WISDOM

subtly surrounding
no need to be introduced
truth without ego

WISHING WELL

instead
of wasting time
wishing ill
on others
make the investment
of wishing well
on yourself.

WORLD BEYOND

the world
sees you
as you see it
your world
shapes the
universe
and the
universe
shapes you

WORTH

always
know your worth
even when
it feels like
everything
has been taken
away
recognize your
presence
realize this
consciousness

YOU CAN LIVE

if you were
someone else
maybe you'd
get yourself
off the shelf
and stop
watching the day
as it slowly
melts away

but you don't
need to be
anyone else
to discover
your true self
and you can start
living the day
instead of letting
it float away

YOUR DREAMS

I know you
were hurt
and that you
wanted revenge

but getting back
didn't work out
like it was
supposed to

and now I hate
to see your dreams
get killed
in this way.

YOUR GAME

you get so paranoid
and subject to comparison
and you get this idea
that others are
having more fun,
perhaps making more money,
and have nicer things,
or are surrounded
by prettier people.

could this be true?
were you really
dealt such a bad hand?
or has your attitude
started to get to you?
this is your game.
why would you waste it
playing someone else's?